Lost Cities

by Rebecca Weber

Table of Contents

Introduction

With the swipe of a **machete** (muh-SHET-ee), the vines hiding the statue fell to the ground. Explorers came face-to-face with a dragon carved out of stone. Behind the vines that had hidden the carving for centuries, they found the wall of a lost city that had been built by a powerful civilization.

For several thousand years, people have built cities. Some cities, once thriving centers, have disappeared completely. A natural disaster, such as an earthquake or a flood, may have buried the city. Or people may have simply moved away, leaving nature to hide the city behind curtains of greenery. In this book, you will learn about four "lost" cities that have been found again.

Mysterious Anasazi ruins can be found at Chaco Canyon in New Mexico.

IT'S A FACT!

Many cultures have stories of ancient ancestors and their lost cities. Usually, these stories are part fact and part fiction. No one knows for sure which is which.

This ancient ruin in Angkor, Cambodia, is well camouflaged by the roots of a tree.

The lost cities you will learn about in this book were built in different places around the world. All of them, once centers of life and work, were abandoned by their inhabitants. In uncovering these cities, we have come to understand more about the civilizations that left them behind.

Chaco Canyon, New Mexico

NORTH AMERICA

CENTRAL AMERICA

SOUTH AMERICA

This map shows the locations of four lost cities.

Machu Picchu, Peru

Pompeii, Italy

Angkor, Cambodia

EUROPE

ASIA

FRICA

AUSTRALIA

Desert High-Rise

The desert sun was bright in Chaco Canyon, an area of what is now New Mexico. It was the spring **solstice**—the day that marks the start of spring. Thousands of people were gathered to celebrate and trade goods. Some had come from the western coast and the lands in what is now Mexico.

People looked forward to the feast of turkey, corn, beans, and squash that had been stored from last fall's harvest. They turned their faces to the warm spring sun and hoped for another year with enough rain to give them a rich harvest.

The people of Chaco Canyon, called the **Anasazi** (an-uh-SAH-zee), lived near the river that sometimes flowed through the canyon. They grew their crops up on the **mesas** (MAY-suhz) that stretched back behind their huge stone houses. They created beautiful artwork and traded with faraway cultures.

That was almost 1,000 years ago. Today, the once-busy centers of Chaco Canyon sit empty and abandoned. Beautiful stone buildings are remnants of their past.

Little by little, **archaeologists** (ark-ee-AHL-uh-jihsts) and **anthropologists** (an-throh-PAHL-uh-jihsts) are learning about the amazing people who built this civilization in the desert and thrived there from 850 to 1250 A.D. They are trying to find out why, after building such an impressive civilization, the Anasazi left it all behind.

These ruins, remains of Anasazi dwellings, tell us how the people of Chaco Canyon lived.

When Spanish explorers traveled through the desert 500 years ago, they thought the abandoned sites they saw were ancient Roman ruins. Later, people believed that the ruins were the remains of Native American peoples. However, the age of the ruins could not be determined.

Then, in the 1930s, scientists proposed that the buildings were at least 1,000 years old. People wondered how the Anasazi had managed to build a civilization so impressive and so unique.

A thriving Anasazi community once occupied this long-abandoned site.

IT'S A FACT!

People of the southwestern desert began farming around 250 A.D. The corn, squash, and beans we eat today are related to the plants these early people developed and grew. The corn originally came from Mexico.

The Anasazi's **ancestors** roamed the plains of North America, following the herds of animals that provided their food. As the people learned to grow crops for food, they no longer needed to roam. They became more settled. They built small villages.

Then, about 1,100 years ago, the Anasazi population began to grow quickly. The people of Chaco Canyon started building cities. Thousands of people lived in the cities. Thousands more lived on the outskirts and considered the closest city their cultural base.

These zigzag pots, found at Pueblo Bonito in Chaco Canyon, are an example of the Anasazi's ingenuity.

For nearly 300 years, Chaco Canyon was the desert's population center. Then, within just a few years, the people left their homes. It appears that they moved quite quickly, leaving valuables and stores of food behind. They may have planned to return.

There are several theories about why the Anasazi left. A **drought** may have made food scarce. A war may have made them feel unsafe. Perhaps a disease killed many of the people and forced the others to flee.

Petroglyphs, such as these, can be found on walls throughout Chaco Canyon. They tell a story, record events, or otherwise document some aspect of Anasazi history.

Some of the Anasazi may have traveled far south to live with the Aztec. Others may have stayed closer to home.

The Pueblo of Arizona and New Mexico have **traditions** that are very similar to those of the Anasazi. Modern Pueblo settlements look much like those that were abandoned in Chaco Canyon. Pueblo art resembles what the Anasazi left behind.

Point

Think About It

"Anasazi" is a Navajo word. It means "ancient ones." Some modern-day archaeologists believe that long ago, the ancestors of today's Navajo fought with the people who lived in Chaco Canyon. Why do you think the two groups of people fought?

in the Kiva Ruins, at Atsinna Pueblo, in Chaco Canyon

City in the Clouds

The Inca people of what is now Peru were very powerful. They ruled much of northern South America when Spanish forces invaded in 1532.

To pay for the huge costs of ruling such a vast area, Incan rulers forced their citizens to pay a labor tax. People could pay this tax by serving in the army, building roads or buildings, or growing food for the empire.

This extraordinary site is Machu Picchu in the Andes Mountains of Peru, South America. Can you see why it is sometimes called the city in the clouds?

One building project was the mountain city of Machu Picchu. The great stone city, built about 550 years ago, took only 10 years to complete.

Archaeologists believe that the city was built as a palace or fortress to keep the emperor safe from enemies. The emperor could come and go as he pleased, but the 1,200 people who lived in the city could not leave it. They spent most of their time working in the service of the emperor. They grew food and kept animals on **terraces**—flat steps of land carved into the mountain. In a city that seemed to float above the clouds, life could be hard for the common people.

The city of Machu Picchu thrived high above the clouds. Then in 1527, the people suddenly packed up their belongings and moved. They came down from their mountain homes and left Machu Picchu to the jungle.

For nearly 400 years, the city sat unknown in the misty clouds. Then in 1911, a local guide led Hiram Bingham, an archaeologist from Yale University, through the jungle and up the steep path to Machu Picchu. Within a year, other archaeologists followed. Under Bingham's direction, **excavations** (ex-kuh-VAY-shuhns) of the hidden city began.

Machu Picchu was, and still is, completely invisible from the valleys below. At the time the Incan people lived there, it could be reached only by climbing thousands of steep stone steps.

To this day, no one knows for sure why Machu Picchu was abandoned. Some archaeologists believe that smallpox, a terrible disease, was the reason. When Europeans invaded North and South America, they brought this disease with them. The native peoples had no natural resistance to the disease, and millions died from it.

Other archaeologists think that Machu Picchu was simply too expensive to maintain. The cost of running the city might have been more than the Incan people could afford, especially at a time when they were dying from disease and warfare.

IT'S A FACT!

The city of Machu Picchu was very well built. There is no mortar between the huge stone blocks of its buildings. Yet the stones are so carefully cut and placed that it's impossible to slip the blade of a knife between them.

the remains of a stone building discovered in 1911

the Royal Tomb of Machu Picchu

Today, Quechua, who are **descendants** of the powerful Incan people, still live in the Andes Mountains. These people make up about half of the population of Peru. Most of them are farmers, raising the same types of crops and animals as their ancestors did.

This city above the clouds is once again an important place in the area. Large numbers of tourists travel there to see the well-preserved ruins of the Incan city. Some people visit the site by train; others hike the old Incan highway for days to reach it.

These hardy tourists walk along the Inca Trail to explore the ruins at Machu Picchu. Under the watchful eye of an alpaca, an animal related to the llama, they experience the wonder of this ancient city's architecture firsthand.

The people of Peru are proud of their city above the clouds. Some want to build a cable car to carry tourists up the mountain to view the sights. Others want to build huge hotels for the visitors. Still others want to preserve the ruins, keeping them as untouched as possible. Whatever its fate, it seems likely that Machu Picchu will never again be lost to the jungle and the clouds.

IT'S A FACT!

The Incan people had no written language. Stories were handed down from generation to generation. When the Spanish came, they stopped the people from telling these stories. The history was lost, and only a few years after the city in the clouds was abandoned, no one knew for sure where it was.

Under the Ashes

The morning of August 24 in the year 79 A.D. was warm and sunny in Pompeii. A light breeze floated through the vineyards and groves of olive trees. People were doing their marketing and selling their goods in this busy Roman seaport.

Pompeii was a place where local farmers could market their crops and livestock. Businesses produced cloth, fish sauce, and millstones, which are large rounded stones used for grinding grain. All of these things were important goods in Roman times.

This fresco painting, called *Harbor Scene*, shows an early view of Pompeii.

The town's **merchants** were rich from trading in wine, oil, and grain. People paid taxes to support their beautiful city, complete with marble statues, flowers, and public baths. The people enjoyed their city and ignored the large, smoking volcano that loomed in the distance. Ten years earlier, a terrible earthquake had seriously damaged much of the town. Pompeii was still at work rebuilding.

IT'S A FACT!

The Roman people who lived in Pompeii scheduled their days around their meals and their trips to the public baths. At the baths, the Romans could bathe in the hot bath (the *calidarium*), the warm bath (the *tepidarium*), or the cold bath (the *frigidarium*).

This undated engraving, depicts citizens of Pompeii enjoying the performance of a puppet player.

19

The Last Day of Pompeii, painted in 1833, depicts the destruction caused by the eruption of Mt. Vesuvius.

Suddenly the peaceful day was shattered by an ear-splitting sound. Pompeii's citizens watched as Mt. Vesuvius exploded, sending a blinding shower of ashes and flaming rocks over the town. Within three days, the town was buried under 15 to 20 feet of ash. Some people managed to escape the flaming rocks and ash. Many more were killed by the eruption.

The destruction was too great for those who had survived to consider rebuilding the city. Silt and ash filled the harbor, making it impossible for boats to enter. Believing that their gods had abandoned the city, most of the people left it, too.

The land where Pompeii had stood eventually recovered from the eruption of Mt. Vesuvius. Some of the survivors who had stayed in the area found their lives to be very different.

No longer living in a rich port city, these people searched for other ways to live. Farmers grew crops in the rich soil. As the years went by, fewer and fewer people remembered the exact site of Pompeii. Eventually, no one knew. Then in 1748, a peasant digging a well in his vineyard struck a buried wall and some beautifully carved marble.

 **Point**

Picture This

Picture the eruption of Mt. Vesuvius. What do you see, hear, smell, feel, and taste? Now draw a picture.

This 1776 painting shows workmen of that time carrying away ash that had buried the Temple of Isis.

21

The Italian government sent trained people to the newly discovered Pompeii to collect the treasures and take them to Italian museums. For 100 years, they concentrated on the main public buildings.

In 1860, government officials ordered a block-by-block excavation of the city. It was eventually decided that the treasures would be left in place and the city would be restored as closely as possible to its original condition.

Today, Pompeii is one of the best-preserved archaeological sites in the world. Frozen in time, it has provided a perfect picture of Roman life at the civilization's peak.

Today, the Forum of Pompeii looks like this, with Mt. Vesuvius in the background.

As archaeologists have excavated and studied the ruins, they have found the remains of more than 2,000 people. The volcanic ash preserved their remains so perfectly that archaeologists have an exact picture of what the people looked like.

Today, many of the descendants of those people who survived the destruction of Pompeii still live in the area. They, too, enjoy the warm weather and the beautiful countryside. Just like their ancestors, they watch and worry about Mt. Vesuvius, smoking in the background.

Archaeologists have found the mummified remains of more than 2,000 people who died when Pompeii was buried.

Towers in the Trees

It was a great city. Its stone **temples** stood tall above the surrounding jungle. It was one of the largest cities in the world, with more than one million people. The people made some of the most beautiful pottery the world has ever known.

This was Angkor, the capital city of the Khmer, who ruled the lands that are now Cambodia, Thailand, Vietnam, and Laos. The Khmer civilization ruled between the 9th and 13th centuries. During that time, Angkor grew to cover more than 144 square miles (400 square kilometers).

Although the Khmer were known for being warriors, Angkor was a peaceful city. People of different religions and backgrounds lived together and prospered.

IT'S A FACT!

The amazing buildings of Angkor are made entirely of stone. The stone was brought in from more than 24 miles (40 kilometers) away. Huge blocks of stone—some larger than a bus—were moved using elephants, buffalo, and human power.

This illustration shows what the doorway to the ruins at Angkor might have looked like.

Today, nearly 900 years after the city's glory days, the temples of Angkor are one of the world's most impressive archaeological sites. Angkor Wat, the main and most famous temple of the city, has been reclaimed from the jungle. People marvel at its enormous size: it covers nearly one square mile (2.8 square kilometers).

Parts of the city still remain covered by jungle. In 1994, the space shuttle *Endeavor* took photographs of the jungles surrounding Angkor. The photographs show many temples and other buildings that remain covered by thick trees and jungle growth.

This temple at Angkor has been completely covered by the trees of the jungle.

The city of Angkor was most prosperous and powerful in the 1100s. Then disease, weak leaders, and enemy invasions slowly drove it into decline. When the city was abandoned for good in 1431, the jungle quickly covered the buildings and began to tear them apart.

The city was rediscovered on January 22, 1860, when French scientist Henri Mouhot found the ruins. For the next 100 years, the French and Cambodian governments worked together to remove the jungle growth and reveal the treasures that remained.

Archaeologists have studied the carvings on the buildings of Angkor in order to learn about its people. The entire city was built around a central pyramid, which was the symbolic home of the gods. The rest of the city was built to look like the gods' actual home. The outer buildings looked like the mountains that the people believed ran around the edge of the sky. Even the reservoirs, **moats**, and canals were built to match the waterways of the gods.

The people who designed Angkor built a large moat around the outside of the city. The moat, which was more than 525 feet (160 meters) wide, flowed in front of the magnificent temple Angkor Wat. In the rainy season it reflected the temple, just like a mirror.

Although Angkor was one of the most powerful cities of its time, its downfall occurred fairly quickly. The royal family fought among themselves, thereby weakening the government. Disease afflicted the people. Enemies who lived in neighboring Thailand invaded in 1431. They conquered the city and then abandoned it.

Within a few years, Angkor was overrun by jungle. People who lived in the region talked about it and wrote about it. However, the city lay undisturbed for nearly 400 years.

Cambodia has had an unsettled history filled with many fierce wars. During the second half of the 20th century, warfare kept archaeologists from entering the country to study Angkor. Battles scarred the buildings and some of the treasures were stolen.

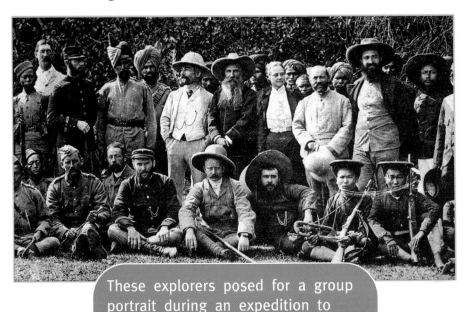

These explorers posed for a group portrait during an expedition to Angkor Wat in 1868.

The people of the world pledged to work together to protect it. Soon there was an international preservation plan to protect the site from further ruin. Now that people are able to study the city, archaeologists are working to learn more about the people who lived there and what became of them.

Carved into Bayon Wall at Angkor is a depiction of a devata, or goddess.

29

Conclusion

Are there other lost cities waiting to be discovered?

Ancient stories tell of a city called Atlantis that disappeared beneath the sea. Was it real? Will it be found?

Is a great city buried under the desert sands of Africa?

Will satellite photos show the outline of an abandoned city in the rain forests of Brazil?

These questions will be answered by archaeologists of the future. Will you be one of them?

Point

Read More About It

Using reference materials, read more about the mysterious disappearance of Roanoke, one of the first English colonies in what is now the United States.

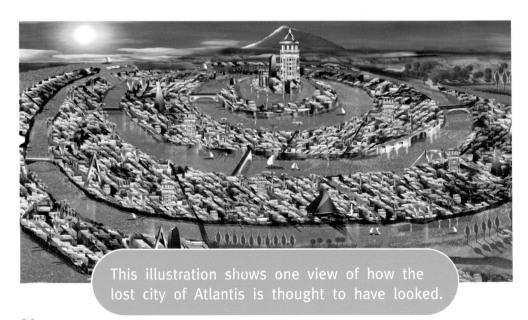

This illustration shows one view of how the lost city of Atlantis is thought to have looked.

Glossary

Anasazi	(an-uh-SAH-zee) an ancient people who lived in the southwestern deserts of what is now the United States (page 6)
ancestor	(AN-sehs-ter) a person's relative who lived in the past (page 9)
anthropologist	(an-throh-PAHL-uh-jihst) someone who studies groups of people (page 7)
archaeologist	(ark-ee-AHL-uh-jihst) someone who studies people of the past through the things they have left behind (page 7)
descendant	(deh-SEND-dent) a person who is related to someone who lived earlier (page 16)
drought	(DROWT) a period with a severe lack of rain or other moisture (page 10)
excavation	(ex-kuh-VAY-shun) the digging out of an archaeological site (page 14)
machete	(muh-SHEHT-ee) a long, curved knife (page 2)
merchant	(MER-chent) someone who sells something (page 19)
mesa	(MAY-suh) a flat-topped mountain (page 6)
moat	(MOHT) a wide ditch filled with water that surrounds a fort or castle, generally used to keep people out (page 27)
solstice	(SOHL-stihs) the day that marks the end of winter and start of spring or the end of summer and start of fall (page 6)
temple	(TEM-puhl) a place where people worship (page 24)
terrace	(TEHR-uhs) flat steps on a hill made for planting or grazing (page 13)
tradition	(truh-DIH-shun) a custom that people follow for generations (page 11)

Index